The Fence Lesson

The Fence Lesson

Poems by

Kay Bosgraaf

Cover design Shay Culligan:

ISBN: 978-1-950462-07-0

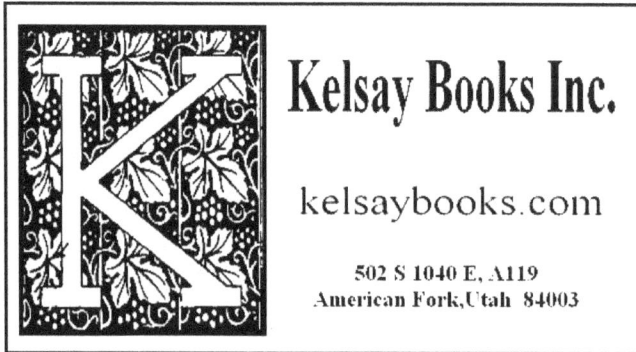

Kelsay Books Inc.

kelsaybooks.com

502 S 1040 E, A119
American Fork,Utah 84003

In Memory of Jessie and John Bosgraaf

Acknowledgments

I am grateful to the editors of the following publications where these poems appeared, many in earlier versions.

In the chapbook *Blue Eyes and Homburg Hats: Poems* published by Presa Press: "Morning Light," "The Fence Lesson," "Overnight on the Farm," "In Autumn Mom and I Drive," "Onion Futures," "Sex-Ed," "After the Calm," "Hiding Places," "My Dad's Claims," "Sunday Dinner After Church at Merna's," "Merna," "Behavior Modification," "My Dad's Position," "Oh, Mother, I Forgot to Tell You," "Jessie Gets Alzheimer's," "Such a Good Girl," "I Will Replace You," "Dinner at Houston's in Georgetown," and "Andrea Bocelli Sings."

Lost Lake Folk Opera Magazine: "Dinner Alone at Ledo's," "Driving Home," and "Onion Futures"
Backbone Mountain Review: "Holy Ghosts in North Carolina," and "Morning Light"
Trancend: A Literary Magazine: "Gynecology"
The Halcyone Literary Quarterly: "Tactical Fear in the City"
The 3288 Review: "The Warrior"
WordWrights: "Jessie Gets Alzheimer's," "My Dad's Position," and "Spring Tease at the Hardware"
Maryland Poetry Review: "I Will Replace You"

I am deeply indebted to Rodney Jones, Lou Lipsitz, Penelope Scambly Schott, Jonathan Giles, and Kay Divant for their careful readings of these poems. The poems have benefitted especially from Barbara Presnell's invaluable insights and her critique of each poem. Thanks also to the MacDowell Colony for their generosity in giving me the time to write the majority of these poems. For the love and support of Richard and my children I will always be grateful.

Contents

I.

A Day in My Summer Playhouse

After breakfast, I clamber through the canvas flaps
and into a large tan tent without a floor

used by my uncles on deer hunting trips in November,
now set up on a grassy patch in the hot sun

between my green shingled house and the sagging
celery-packing shed. I fold the flaps over each other

to close myself off from the farm help walking by.
The vapors of the musty canvas collect around me.

I pick up my baby doll from her tiny bed, sit down
on the grass to take off her blue dress, slip, and panties,

open and close her eyes with my finger, poke her navel,
put her in pink panties and sleeper, wrap her neatly

in a flannel receiving blanket covered with tiny teddy
bears. I fill her bottle from my bucket of water, slide

the tiny rubber nipple into her mouth. After my baby
finishes, I change her panties, I might give her a bath

and then a nap. I hear some men laughing loudly,
pull aside the tent flap and see several of them throwing

baby birds against the barn. I don't know why. Later
I look at some of the babies fallen to the ground. Their

downy feathers barely cover them. They have wide
open orange beaks, just the right size for my dolly's bottle.

I Watch Uncle Al Work

I smile at my blue-sky morning in Michigan.
The doorway leads to the backyard and the black
fields being plowed in this morning light, sunny

and tender, clean blue sky. I go out and walk
to the edge of the field to better see the large
boned work horses yoked to the plow.

Up on the wooden plank seat Uncle Al
with his large rough hands holding the reins
smacks the horses' rumps and hollers at them

to keep moving up the field. The planting will begin
after another day's work when the plowed furrows
are made smooth by the same team pulling

a flat wooden drag over the field up and down.
He works the team all morning, then drives them
to the barn to be put up for the day. I follow him

into the barn with its rafters, dark corners, and watch him
brush the sweaty horses, feed and water them—
Notice the stink of the horses, their curious droppings

falling in heaps, how they urinate with such force—
A bulb casts its dim light down into the room
with its few dirty windows, illuminating the webs

and trapped bugs. He sets me high up
on one of the warm and gentle creatures,
talks to them as he goes about his work.

The Fence Lesson

We walk up the hill and down over the long brown grass
of the meadow to the gully and the fence.

Grandpa Hoek stands beside me, gently explains
how the electricity keeps the cows from breaking through

to the washed-out trenches of the gulley. His face
kind and sweet like my mother's, he stands tall and large

while I, no higher than the fence. Silence and freezing cold
all around us, he tells me I can touch it.

Through my wooly thick mitten, I feel painful electric currents
and I do not cry but I wonder why he told me to do that

and I think he was not playing a trick on me but teaching me
a cow lesson and then I wonder what other kinds

of lessons he is going to teach me.
The red barn gleaming in the sun seems far away.

Overnight on the Farm

Before breakfast I slowly feel my way through the crowded,
cold, and musty storage room at the back of the house

to the sink and toilet in the far corner. My toothbrush
is still wet from the night before and I can see mold

building on the edges of the sink. One bare bulb dangles
above me at the end of a cord. When I walk into the kitchen,

still shivering from the unheated back room, I see the sticky
fly paper spiraling down from the ceiling where dead flies

cluster. A full milk can brought in from the barn stands
near the work table. Aunt Doris takes a large spoon and skims

the cream risen to the top. Next she ladles the milk into a glass
to serve me with breakfast in the dimly lit dining room.

The milk, smelling sour, tastes warm and revolting. Outdoors
life is brighter, the back porch sunny where I warm myself

before I walk into the barn and find a large wooden
bin filled with grains of wheat, sit deeply into it, and let

the granules stream through my fingers, cool and surprising.

Each Fall, Mom and I Drive

No other cars within hearing, only the quiet
on this warm day, windows rolled down, the scent
of turning leaves. The narrow dirt road winds

through the woods, my mom driving
and I in the back seat watching out the side windows,
both of us hoping for low hanging limbs

on the passing trees, waiting to spot leaves
wine red and gleaming gold around a curve
or along a stretch ahead. We stop.

Mom breaks off small branches, hands them over
until I am buried in the radiance of this rustling.

Onion Futures

If we needed a break, we walked to the edge
of the onion field to the old hand pump, prime it,
cup our hands and drink in the shade
of the willow tree. My twelve-year-old eyes
saw so many onions in a long day in the sun
that at night I dreamed about onions rolling
in great streams and waterfalls making me dizzy
in my sleep.

Michigan onions are ripe for harvest
in August, acres of neat rows of gray-green
spikey tops in the hot wind urging us cousins
to drop to our knees, tug at a clump,
lift it from the rich black soil. Holding
a bunch in my left hand, I take my foot-long
shears and slice through the tops letting
the onion heads thump and bounce in the bottom
of a wooden crate whose slats are weathered gray
from years of being filled with onions over and over.
We four keep at it, the onions slowly piling up
rounding off the crates.

Earning ten cents a crate to spend at the county
fair, we ride the tilt-a-whirl, the Ferris wheel,
feel our stomachs in our throats, walk slowly
through the freak house, pluck at our pink cotton
candy, all to the exciting music of the merry-go-round
and the carneys shouting. We use the rest room
where a woman sits on a chair with a bowl
of nickels and dimes on the counter in front of her.
Clutching my new teddy bear, I walk home alone
down the dark country road past the onion fields
lit by the moon that casts my shadow beside me.

Sex-Ed

I sex-eded myself when I was roller skating
with Bertram holding me close around my waist
with his warm arm, our legs in perfect sync gliding,
he maneuvering me gently around and around
the rink. I was fourteen in the eighth grade
and went all twitchy for the first time. No longer
aware of him—only of myself and my
swelling body—I loved it, my body, the roller
rink, the organ music—mystery and secret.

Soon enough I had more sex-ed sitting in the front
seat of Harry's car—his hand slowly roaming
my leg moving up my calf encased with knee high
navy-blue socks, my thighs, plaid wool Bermudas.
I did not like him and he had not kissed me
or even flirted, not even with his eyes. But
his hand kept crawling up on our first date and I
was fifteen. So I slid over, opened the car
door, stepped out, and strolled into my house.

After the Calm

As that warm Sunday moves towards cooling
dusk, the black dust swept by the hot wind
for the past three days lies quietly settled
by a steady rain, a real soaker, my father says,

as the rain stops and the sky clears.
He sits in his mission oak rocker in the darkening
porch sipping his Old Milwaukee, he offers me
a taste of the foam on top. He wears only

his trousers and sleeveless undershirt.
Few cars drive by our house. Then the evening
is awakened by the screaming of the neighbors'
newborn baby. My father rears himself up

from the rocker, stands close to the screened window
behind his chair, and repeatedly hollers past
the stars and the moon, "Shut that kid up!" My mom
shushes him from the kitchen. I hate the taste of foam.

My Dad's Claims

I am from the Dutch and Frisian
I am from farm work and child labor
I am from my father's belt
From his rage
I am from the eighth grade
I am from the black soil
From calluses on my hands
From sharp knives and celery plants
From weeds and weed killer
From conveyer belts and packing plants
I am from fixing tractors and engines and planters
I am from ditch dredging and fixing the irrigation
I am from intelligence and being smart

I am from blue eyes and Homburg hats
From hot rods and Harleys
I am from plow horses and stock car races
From power boats and water fights
From brothers and sisters

I am from making stilts and buying bikes
I am from joking and laughing
I am from rocking on the sun porch and having a beer
From good food
From neighbors like me
From making things right again

My Dad's Position

Now in his grave, his bones lie quietly,
his hands still folded over his dark blue suit,

his left hand cupped around his right hand
to shape his crooked index finger

that would not bend at the first knuckle,
his pale cheeks conformed to his jaw now slack,

a jaw that was never slack behind his chilling
commands when he jabbed that forefinger

on the kitchen table to yell, to admonish,
to order—go to hell, stay or get what's coming to you.

And once, slumped in his easy chair he pointed
toward the birch grove down the road where his neighbor

deliberately placed himself in his Oldsmobile
and swallowed its exhaust. After he told us,

my dad smirked, his wiry arms resting,
his hands folded across his belly's soft arc.

Oh, Mother

I forgot to tell you I noticed
      when he poked fun of you.

Noticed when he criticized your cooking,
      how you bowed your head at the dinner table
      to pick at your cuticles when you couldn't eat.

I heard you crying as you sat in the car on our shopping trip
      to buy you a new dress. (You chose the teal knit
      that made you look so soft.)

I stood outside the locked bathroom door when you
      went there to sob.
      You ached for so many years.

I forgot to tell you that you were a stoic role model.
      That you were warm and welcoming to my friends,
      That I always knew you loved me. That I thrilled
      to your warm hands massaging my back and arms.

Oh, Mother...
      I wish I could have soothed you all those years.

When I was ready, you had long before been lost
      in Alzheimer's forest.

My Mother's Hiding Place

When I pull up my tights and finger the wide run
straight up to my navel, I remember my mother's
brown scar from her hysterectomy in the same place

on her stomach, like a zipper to let someone in or out,
the pink skin on either side soft and lumpy,
the muscle sliced in half years before.

She, tender, warm, and soft, I now want back into her womb—
to be unaware of the wretched in this hateful world—
the mutilation, always the wounds.

When I was a child, she sang her way through every day—
frying the bacon, mopping the floor, changing the beds—
the songs were her womb to rest in—

those old country hymns—"Rock of Ages,"
"On a Hill Far Away," "Jesus Keep Me Near the Cross"—
dozens of them, her rich alto swells—low to high—

up and down—echoing those days of hard work
and rough times—four brothers in the Pacific,
what she knew of Jewish internment,

the Nazis in the Netherlands, my father's rants.
To extinguish the violence, she sang—*Sing, Mom, Sing!*
No more trouble now—sing the hell out of it all.

Jessie Gets Alzheimer's

In July my mom sat across the table from me,
told how safe she was in her house, she did not need to move.

After all, huge guards roamed her yard at night,
she told between sips of tea from her Johnson Brothers cup,

her lips trembling, hands shaking, the house hot
because she turned the furnace up that warm Michigan day.

So in December my daughters and I drove the 500 miles again,
to her new room in the home, sat on her new blue couch,

she across from us in her maple rocking chair, smiling,
asking the girls who their mother was and were they sisters

and they too kept smiling, looking steadily into her dark
hazel eyes, her permed hair wildly sticking out, smears of blush

on her cheeks. Then I saw into her bathroom, the soiled
tissue folded into a little square and carefully placed

on the floor next to the toilet. I saw where she wrote her name
on the glossy white wall in shaky capital letters in blue ink

at an angle—J-E-S-S-I-E. Soon it will be July again
and now she wears Depends, sometimes smells of urine,

refuses to sleep in her bed preferring a winged back chair
near the station for the women working the night shift.

When I go to bed, I see her there, ankles swelling, bend over her,
lift her feet to the hassock.

Such a Good Girl

As we hug good-bye she articulates,
"You're such a good girl," a complete

sentence even though her frontal lobe
is filled with wormy squiggles, little

springs of crazy making, little bits
of devastation taking charge of her

past and present, the brain turned
into a honeycomb, a porous shrunken

chunk like a sponge, not one that absorbs
and holds, but one dried up past parsing

knowledge into new understandings
no longer connected logically but logical

nevertheless. For God's sake, Mom,
you stood there holding a one-dollar bill

and told me you wanted to give me four ones
for my troubles. "You're such a good girl."

Uncle Tim's Stroke

The power of electricity spiked
through his brain, a lightning bolt
from the leather pouch at Zeus's

feet where he kept his store.
This cooperative and steady god
got him, split that brain into halves

and dropped him to the ceramic floor
in front of his toilet, fell from group
reasoning to be an individual thinker

who lives within himself in a home
of others who live within themselves
in special mental spaces with special

privileges. Not thinking clearly,
he loses his cell phone, a white tennis shoe,
red golf shirt, rides his bike down the middle

of the street, asks strangers for money,
cigarettes, and chocolates. Cheese curls,
now his special reward for polite talk,

no more yelling or bullying his roommate.
He still bullies her with what remains, not the boys
his children, but her, he will always bully her.

This time there are consequences, no cheese curls
for you, bully man. This grown man gets
scolded—you may not yell at Bill you must

eat your dinner you must take your pills
or no more cheese curls to give to bully man.
Poor bully man. Cry for bully man.

Merna's Sense of Humor

I admire proud Merna, a widow with six children,
new in my hometown. Together they fill

an entire mahogany pew in my church.
Merna drives a Fiat, not much larger

than a big club chair, for the commute
to her teaching job in a private school.

She says she was hired on the basis
of two hard years of teachers' college in Iowa.

She values education and correct English
grammar and ridicules those who don't know

the rules. Merna laughs and loves her children.
Often I stay over with her two girls

in their double bed—twelve limbs all finding a place—
or I sleep on the living room couch

around the corner from Merna's bedroom.
I hear her in the middle of the night

get up to use the bathroom,
hear her knock loudly against some object

and then exclaim, "You stupid cow."
Unknown to her, I am there just out of

sight. I grin and love the name she calls herself.
I did not know a mom could be that funny.

After Church at Merna's

I am seated at her dinner table, antique walnut pulled
out with as many leaves as it will take, covered

with white linen damask—a guest of her daughter,
my best friend. Others sit, too, five more of her own

children, two friends of the older boys—nine children,
most of us teenagers—laughing, hollering, teasing—

and Merna. Never knowing ahead how many there will be,
when she sits down and starts the procession of serving

platters and dishes, she prays there will be enough chicken.
When the boy sitting next to her hesitates to take

the last meaty piece, she says, "No, no, no. You
take the breast and let me have the back.

It's my favorite piece." She grins at the noisy commotion
and helps herself to the best four bites of the entire bird.

Behavior Modification

Oh, Merna. I want to be like you,
my ideal grown-up—educated, a teacher,

strong woman, great sense of humor.
Then I will be good enough—not just the teenage

daughter of parents who are locals, like weeds,
and a father who yells and scares me away.

I hide from him, afraid he will hurt me,
someday kill me. I am three and he raises

his fist at me. I am four and he ridicules
my mom at supper time. I am five

and he screams at me from the front seat
of the Oldsmobile because I lost

a copper pin: "You'd lose your ass
if it wasn't tied to you." During this vacation

I find my mom sitting alone in the daytime darkness
of the tiny house trailer. She cries, tears running down,

and sobs, "He don't mean nothing by it."
He yells at her from outside, "Shut up your damn

crying in there. You ain't no baby!"
Is her chest crashing and hurting to cry like this?

I back away. I am too young to help her.
I feel separate from her. I don't know

to crawl away. As a teenager I feel shades
of this darkness when Merna has a good laugh

about locals who talk like my parents. She laughs
with her children about these ignorant ones

imitating their sounds and words—she don't, he don't,
I ain't gonna—hah hah hah. Merna knows my mom and dad.

She needs to shove me into a downward spiral
when she laughs.

I Will Replace You

I will buy my own sail boat
a 30 foot Catalina,
learn to put up the jib,
to pilot, to take control.

The jenny will slice my boat
through the turbulence and in light winds.
My Baltic blue spinnaker
will gently puff out and always take me forward.
I will not be dead in the water.

I will have a small brick town house,
two bedrooms, one bath,
with a wood burning stove in the living room,
hardwood floors, rag rugs,
a pie safe,
quilts on my walls—in every room,
Amish solids—navy, forest green, dark red—
And on my new bronze bed, soft yellow.

All three children will come home with friends
and I will cook and bake like I never have before.
They will swoon over my Thanksgiving turkey
and love my summer pasta salads.

I will have a home
with a lover in my bed
who will kiss my eyelids,
my neck, breasts, belly, rest his face there.
The joints of the metal bed will groan
as we nibble around each other's mouths
like small fishes nibble sea weed in the bay,
meld our skin with sweat.

Dinner at Houston's in Georgetown

When the waiter asks me what I want, I think
of my daughter who is standing me up at a time

in my life when I need a little role reversal
so I can be mothered. I hope she can be here

tonight sitting across from me as I expected.
I need to be soothed and know I expect too much.

After an hour, when she does not show, I think
of catching the eye of one of the four men

at the next table. But I see those bulbous aging
noses and realize a one-night triste would make me

bone weary, so I wait for her at my table set for two.

Black Hog Barbeque

Waiting for my daughter
to arrive, I slide over
in the booth into the sun

so Black Hog's air conditioning
does not cause goose bumps
on my arms—like on a freshly

defeathered chicken, the whole
bird resembling a newborn
baby, her little bottom

the right size to place in the palm
of my left hand while I support
her head for some nuzzling

before a nurse plucks her up,
bathes, diapers and swaddles her,
as I wait for my daughter.

Andrea Bocelli Sings

His sacred aria fills me with hope. My chest swells
with deep breaths, Christmas is almost here

and I am southbound on the Carolinian. Bocelli
reminds me of my high school concert choir—

the recording session, the red plastic 78 rpm kept
for more than thirty years and then lost when we divided

our possessions. No beautiful sounds remained
because I was deaf to them. For too many years

at Christmas all of its decorations served as large fish
hooks snagging on the recent past. The porcelain

angel topping the tree and the tree itself sent me back
to opening gifts with him. The train stops

in Petersburg and my mind jerks back again. Here
he said he was leaving me. Here began my journey

submerged in desperation. We begin moving again,
and I remember what is near—my new Christmas

angel of flesh and bone with blond hair and blue eyes—
sweet baby Lucy who is learning her first words

will come to see the "choo-choo." She will hug me
and pat my cheeks. The white pine forest opens a path,

the fog makes way for the sun, and the train thunders on.

The Hunt

I would be mad for a coat made of red fox—
but I would treasure a coat of muskrat

like cousin Tom trapped in watery ditches
between the icy fields to sell for coats.

Once when we were kids I checked the iron traps
with him, watched him pry one open,

release the small dead animal into a burlap
bag with the others to sell to the furrier.

And I would cherish a raccoon coat
made from pelts Uncle Ollie strung up,

stinking and waiting for a furrier to come.
My dad passed along his stories of the hunt

while I watched the hounds in their runs
race back and forth, barking and howling

just as they did when they drove a raccoon
up a tree. I can still hear them—ahhh ouuu.

I froze in my fabric jacket.

Now I will hunt for a warm coat, an early raccoon
with large shoulder pads and cuffed sleeves,

full length, and never be as cold as when I walked home
up Van Buren Street into the Michigan winter.

II.

What Eggs Do

An egg—a brown egg—once covered
with feces—so far from the hen who laid

it—a perfect oval—a perfect weight and fit
for the palm of my hand—so comforting,

an egg, a brown egg—apparently the result
of a rooster crowing and carrying on proudly

in the chicken yard—his radiant colors
in contrast to the white feathers of the small hen—

a soft comfort to the chicks she hides
under her wings. An egg for breakfast—an egg

beaten in an omelet—blue egg in a robin's nest—
mottled in a hawk's nest—an egg to become a baby

in the uterus—an egg that does not merely float
around and allow a sperm to penetrate her

when he wants—but an egg with grabbers to grab
a sperm—like a catcher snatching a baseball.

She takes charge of him—acts mightily to become
fertilized. Such is the way of the egg—

No matter how the cock crows.

A Broken Baby Boy

I believed it when I read it—that the mother
had allowed her boyfriend to beat one of her infant twins

because the baby boy resembled his father.
This bothered the boyfriend so he cracked the baby's

skull and broke his bones. The baby boy will not return
to lie by his sister, never run with ease, never sing

in the church choir, never snuggle in bed with Harry
Potter, never take home an A in sixth grade, never

meet the boyfriend serving five-to-ten for beating
his mother, never know how to hate or forgive.

Dinner Alone at Ledo's Pizza

I look up when I hear a hollow thump
and know that the father in the next booth has stuck

his fist into one of his three girls. Violent movies, solid hits
on the back have taught me this sound. After

the thump, I hear perfect silence and then a mournful
scream bursts from the toddler sitting next to him.

Facing her and him, I see her try to catch her breath
as he says, "I told you not to stand up." She wanted

to see who was sitting behind her. "Be quiet. Stop
crying. I said, Stop crying now." She gasps for air

as she tries to still her sobs, tries to obey him and finally
quiets herself as her sisters watch from across the table.

"Sit up straight in your seat," he says to another one.
"Sit up straight or we'll have to leave and I'll tell

your mother. Sit up straight." If dad uses his fisted voice
and hand, I wonder what mom will use. I want to tell one

of his girls to kill him in his sleep. Soon he leaves
with his three disheveled ones lagging behind,

one still clutching her slice.

Zimmer Woman

Give me the powers of the great bird of love,
The Zimmer. Give me flight back

to when I was a young mother with preemie baby twins
and waning energy. Let me do it again with Zimmer

bird vigor. Then I would not need naps. Diapers
would be washed, folded and smelling of sunshine.

Little dresses and rompers would hang ironed just so
and sleepers, stacked neatly in the drawer. Always

enough clean swaddling blankets. Glass bottles
with two kinds of baby formula would line the refrigerator—

half with pink caps, half with blue, all topped
with preemie nipples. My arms would not tire

from coddling one baby, then walking the other,
soft skin and plush hair warm against my cheek.

In the night, I would do the feedings every two hours,
and not feel ready to collapse. With the Zimmer

bird's power, I would feel fresh in the morning
for their breakfast and baths, nap them, feed them,

nap them, feed them and at four rock one on each shoulder
during their fussy time. Feeding again and at last to bed.

Oh, I wish I had been like the great bird of love.
I would have said, Hello, Babies, I am your powerful

mother, I am Zimmer Woman.

"Sleep tight.
No harm tonight,
In starry skies
The Zimmer flies."

After poet Paul Zimmer

The Pied Piper

A knock on the door. A high school girl
with an even voice asks, Do you know

your children are on the grass in the middle
of the street? And then she is gone. She means

the grass in the fork bounded by D.C.'s
New Hampshire Avenue. How did my two-year-old

twins get there? Who let them out of the back yard
secured by a picket fence. Eight months pregnant,

shoeless, I race out the door and down the sidewalk,
across the street, and grab their plump arms.

Cars and buses speed by us as we cross back.
Once home, standing in front of me in their red jumpsuits

and staring at me with their big blue eyes, their shocked faces
reflect the fear in my shaking voice and many hugs.

On my knees before them I listen with all the love
in my heart pounding while they explain in their own

way. Kitty! Kitty! How they pushed aside a loose picket
and followed their soft, fuzzy to the grassy mound.

Five Years a Good Patient

Sometimes my daughter's voice is low
and then I know her body's trigeminal nerve
again is sending hot electrified needles

through her jaw, creating an unrelenting
burning in her gums, not a cure or treatment,
but a scorching so intense that she covers

her face with ice packs as she scrunches
down further under her bed covers
as if trying to hide from her body's

torture. She can only exist in a bleary
consciousness from the medications
which do not numb the pain. No help, no

relief. The whoosh of her friends' hellos
from her iPhone will not pierce through her
defenses this day. Consumed by the fire,

she isolates herself from her son, daughter,
husband. Towards evening she will emerge,
kiss her children good night, go into the garage

to smoke medicinal pot, and try to watch
a movie with her husband before a restless
night and the next day's fight for her life.

With a tentative smile, she told me such
pain is called the suicide disease. Is she
warning me even as she promises to stay alive?

In the Hospital's Waiting Room

This page smells of medicine
and it's dark in the waiting room.
How long does brain stem surgery take?

Warning to my daughter: You will be
a quadriplegic if a mistake is made.
If it works, the pain will be gone.

I feel like screaming at the screaming baby
in the next room, but I sit
like a mummy with no expression,
no words for anyone.

Many voices mix together—throaty—
buttons—disease—bye bye—thank you—wait—
voices distinguished by words but no sense.
Woman wearing red lipstick
tapping her foot—

Receptionists sit behind the glass window,
Chatting in hushed tones. I hear the word dying.
Don't let it be my child.

The one in a yellow shirt is the loudest—
I want to tell them to shut up, grab the foot
of the woman to stop the tapping—
Yack yack screeching baby
Why isn't someone tending that baby?

Don't let her die. Don't let the knife sink.
Be precise when cutting the nerve in six places.

The Warrior

Imagine the girl thirteen years old and small for her age,
pitching forward from her backpack's weight, auburn hair
bouncing. She pushes down the sidewalk into the dark
to her babysitting job several long blocks from her home—
out of hearing, out of sight.

Imagine him, heavy, muscular, medium height, easing
up the street in his old blue Honda and seeing no one else,
stops, gets out to ask for directions. He claps his rough hand
over her mouth, shoves her into his idling car, speeds off.

Imagine she has a vision of victory. How to do it.
Her Tae Kwon Do training bellows at her to break his thick
neck just as she can break three boards with her hand.
But he restrains her arms in the bucket seat, tightens his hold.
He stops the car in the woods behind the mall, yanks her out.

Imagine her giving him a side kick in the groin, and he jerks
back. She, slamming her heel like a steel hammer into his shin,
pulls out of his weakened grasp and runs as fast as Joan of Arc
riding at a gallop. The man hobbles after her. She leads him
unfettered, unflinching.

Imagine all glory. Imagine no fire.

Summer Camp at Montgomery College

The brown plastic park bench feels like human
cheeks covered with deep red acne scars.

My ninth and tenth grade students fill a classroom
and wait for me—I cannot stay in my escape bower

any longer but must go in and face them. What do they think
of a sixty-year-old woman with sun spots on her hands,

a soft stomach, arms beginning to flab? I think they see
through me, that I'm in this summer class for the money

and burnt out from another semester of grading papers.
Who are they behind their scrubbed faces and braces,

clean T-shirts and jeans? They look so well taken care of,
are polite and bright, full of imagination. But they talk

about being forced to do laundry and take the bus. How trite
they are, I think, until they write about lazy mothers

and loud hollering fathers, depression and suicide. At first they
looked ripe for challenging creative writing assignments

but my lack of energy holds them back and now they sit
looking bored. They are reflecting what they see in me.

We would rather be at the beach.

Last Night I Dreamed

A favorite student
comes to me to show me a pencil drawing
on both sides of a white sheet of paper
Tells me he has drawn me
The paper flashes back and forth in his hands
On one side an abstract soft woman
with little babies in clusters in balloons
in different parts of her body
most in her large uterus some in her breasts
tucked here and there in several places
She is drawn large
hair, limbs
I am that woman in his mind
fertile nourishing
She has a monumental presence
No, that's not you, he says
And on the other side
an ample figure again
another fecund female
heavy and smiling
and I say I like how he has drawn me
and he says, no that isn't you
and he points to a tiny figure
near the right foot of the towering figure
at the edge of the paper
A gray old woman sitting
at a desk hunched over concentrating
a stern look on her pointed face, dull hair
That's you, he says, right there.

Simple Wish

The chill on my back from the large plate glass wall
reminds me that winter is nearly here,

the late afternoon drizzle like snow, palpable but not rain,
the lamps not yet on outside. I shiver when I look

through the interior glass wall of the classroom
and see the neon cylinders suspended from the ceiling—

an amusing center space but all hard surfaces and light
that suggests more cold. Soon this writing workshop

will end and I will be on my way. I want to get home
to be with Molly, my Old English sheepdog,

to settle on the floor with her, absorb her warmth,
scratch her tummy when she rolls onto her back

and looks at me. I love her soft beard and downy hair
on her ears. Not needing to be charmed

into knowing she is valued, Molly licks my hand, tells me
she loves me, kisses my cheek, and makes me laugh.

Driving Home in the Dark after Class

At dark two police cars—red blue swirls
siren whorls—slide horizontally across
four lanes of traffic toward the chilly concrete
barrier—park before the old blue panel van
with sunken front end from the hit in cold November

in the red blue swirls
a dozen people in winter jackets
slouch around—traffic slows
an officer proceeds north on foot
along the concrete barrier

up the median gun glinting
in the headlights of eight lanes
from ahead and behind,
then the partner, gun in hand, follows backing him up
miasma of red, blue, white—the doe leads them

as fast as her percussive legs allow
up the highway median beside the gray chill barrier
two strong front legs haul her body
hobbled hind legs trail
in the strobe of red and blue swirls

one officer behind the other in their tan uniforms
her soft tan fur and thick white tail
she still leads with two legs dangling
hooves clack in their raggedy dance
joints and feet point this way and that

soon a pointed metallic sphere will breach her fur
echo off the barrier past
the cold red swirls
and into the waiting woods

The Singer

After the night of rain, the mockingbird
sits in the clean air on the highest branch—
the dead one—of the Indian cigar tree

and clearly pipes her songs, perfect
in her imitations of many birds. Not
a bad way to live, I think. If a song

can be a lovely imitation of another's,
is it of less value because it is not one's own?
If that is the best one can do? Isn't this bird's

warble as beautiful as the song she first heard?
Or is the mockingbird a forger and thief
to be derided for her uncanny ability?

No. This notable bird has a great time, is always
ready to perform, and never hides her sources,
a bird as scrupulous as the finest scholar.

III.

Preening

The wild turkey displays himself outside the woods,
his fan tail circled wide like a peacock's, but the bird is brown

and his body resembles an armadillo on sticks—not a pretty fowl.
The tail is his saving grace with its yellow band

inches from the edge, following around. I can see
he is proud, this male turning his tail towards the woods

and freezing in one pose to tempt the unadorned females
with his shades of brown and pure gold gleaming in the sun.

An unsung sense of order floats above him, omen
that an amazing primal urge waits as the final explanation.

Diving In

We spoke on the phone and decided to meet.
Seeing you for the first time, I liked your height
and graying auburn hair, pleasant smiling face—

sure of yourself. Our first date—Thanksgiving
dinner at Mary's house—had begun. Driving
to her house, I was anxious.

When Mary asked us all to hold hands and name
one thing that made us thankful, I was self-conscious,
but you seemed at ease. I liked the touch

of your warm hand. As turkey, dressing, spoon bread
and all the dishes were passed, you were amusing.
Later when I drove you home, I wondered how our evening

might end. You invited me in. I had my moment to leave
but I chose to go in. I could have sat on a chair,
but instead sank into your gray couch close to you

where we talked about what we hoped for in a relationship.
I was still nervous. You said you wanted to be settled.
You wanted someone who wanted you.

Now I was under your spell. Later in bed I discovered
your surprising middle-aged body—lithe, slim, long, warm.
We fit together like two puzzle pieces—our bodies lay

against each other's in a way I had never known before,
such delicate touching. My doubts assuaged, I dove
into our relationship like a sleek Olympic swimmer

who has yet to come up for air.

At Rik's

We are out for dinner, I savor
my martini and you, a glass

of merlot, I with my roasted rice
bowl, you, crab cakes. Playing footsie

under the high table, our eyes
meet as we talk about nothing

and fill me as surely as scorching
love making. When we leave, you lay

your hand on the small of my back,
a more potent gesture than any kiss.

Our Ghost Harry

Almost one year gone, yet in this house your fur
still clings to Richard's black tuxedo in the closet,
your ashes now spread between the apple trees
in a Williamsport orchard, apple picking time

already come and gone. You float, a ghostly sheepdog
wending around the trees, curious about your new home
like the bold Old English you were.
During your last days, you lay as a limp puddle of fur

on the floor at the far end of the kitchen,
not sitting at attention between us waiting
for a crumb to drop as we ate our dinner.
You got old and sick, my lovely friend.

I miss the great wops of your large paws on my legs,
you wanting my attention, your kisses on my arms,
hands, face—always giving and giving kisses.
And now we've given you back to God. Your ashes

mix with rain to percolate into the luscious decay
of fallen apples. From this fertile soil your sweet
ghost will spring when you hear us walk
through the orchard and you meander with us.

Soft as Fur

The fur around the edge of the hood
of his new Christmas jacket suits
him. He is soft as a kitten, loves

to snuggle, to touch—his warm
hand holding mine as he slowly
runs his finger down my palm—

his breath on my face inviting me
to come closer—to nuzzle, explore
lips and mouths—so short the time

to play—the final hug too firm
to suggest anything more before
he rushes out the door.

No Stopping Allowed

He insists his body is slowing down—his birthday
is next month, so what do I expect, he asks, but I tell him
his body does not have to become slack and sluggish
if he goes to the gym, if he walks farther than he now

walks the dog, that he must do more because age steals
muscle tissue even if we are aware of it. (I do not tell
him that his arms are getting scrawny and his back shows
a slight stoop.) He says I nag him—that gyms and exercise

have never been his thing. If I gave him a hawk and a moor,
he would show me how fast he can run. So I will plan walks,
let him lug in all the firewood and groceries, together
map out hiking trips to track down all of the waterfalls

in Washington County because I will not allow his legs
and heart to diminish to fragility, feebleness, a slow-pace
that stops him. His thick hair is silvery blond, the same shades
of white and gray as our Old English sheepdog's fur. His face

serene and not wrinkled, he still writes twelve-hours a day,
fifteen one day last week, and he bragged this morning
that he has not lost any of his words, that they all come to him
when he needs them—at least within the hour, he admits.

Jacksonville Beach Makeover

At the beach finally, a long time coming, I wake to a view
of silent waves curling under themselves, folding and unfolding
in the sun but I hear only the air conditioner. I kiss Richard
goodbye, gather my bags to get out of this closed in room and onto
the sand, to listen, to lie on my towel in my jade suit, my work-
tense body to settle into the warmth.

A deeply tanned vendor sets up a turquoise umbrella and I
stay on my stomach, resting on my elbows reading, then doze in
the warm morning, waves slushing softer louder over and over.

The August day continues to heat up the warm sand against
my feet so I move to the water and cool down with quick fish-like
motions and emerge to drip off slowly onto my beach chair as I
watch a dad smooth sun screen on his toddler's back and then
follow the boy as he races from the water's edge—sometimes
filling his red shovel with water to carry back to his dad but mostly
squatting just short of the waves.

I flip back to my *Vogue*—what I want, the stasis I need.
Noticing indistinct radio sounds scratch through cheap amplifiers, I
glance up and watch children who look like middle schoolers run,
holler, their parents following in slow motion.

Soon noon comes, my feet protesting now out beyond the
edge of the shade. I study a seagull bathing in a shallow pool
brought in by the waves. Just like I love to do, this bird jumps each
wave when it comes in, another and another, then settles into
bathing again, until another series of waves comes in.

Just then, Richard, fully dressed in khakis, shirt, and shoes, finds me to go have the seafood lunch that we both crave. We sit outside where we have a view of flowers and plants separating us from the street. The oysters and wine are great but I catch myself longing to get back to my chair and umbrella.

After lunch I nap and wake to three young women in their shiny bikinis standing in a small circle chatting and laughing, tossing a volleyball between them, their skin taut and tanned. An elderly couple sitting near me watch, appear to absorb the vigor. I loaf and leaf through the magazine featuring fall clothes, even furs. I breathe in the fresh salt air, take a walk to put some color on my pale shoulders, lose some stomach.

Purged by the water and the sun, I feel the release of the tightness in my neck—rejuvenate now, notice the pleasure, health, and energy—this is all, pay attention now—the water like silk swirling—a light khaki green giving way to a darker shade and then a nearly black ocean dazzles like diamonds against the blue sky laced with white haze.

I swim again, jump the waves, not letting them push me around, smack me over or under. With tired muscles in my legs, I go back to my chair and stretch as the shadows lengthen and families wander off the beach, the little boy with the red shovel lagging behind while a group of young people begin a game of beach volleyball. I prop up my feet and read an article, sit until I see a swath of dark gray water, a reminder of the riptides to come when we walk the beach tonight.

When the tide comes creeping in, I pack up to go back to my room where Richard waits for me—with an ocean view, silent waves, and air conditioning. Together we climb the stairs to the rooftop lounge where breezes blow, the ocean sighs from the shore, and we raise our glasses in a toast. Cheers!

My Sweet Love

I will tell you what I want to consume
after a meal—dark winter evenings,

a secret red song we share, your soft skin
smelling of mint and spices.

Desire seeps into my body like honey
into hot tea, like the heat of warm bricks

under cold bare feet. This is home,
to be rooted to the earth, held

down by the solid goodness of you,
protected from the pull of the moon.

After Six Weeks

Leaving you alone at Mayo Clinic, I clamber into the cold airport
van to Minneapolis. A lone house stands in a fenced area
beside a leaning gray barn, pile of hay, tall silos, then a family-
owned motel, little Oscar's restaurant, gas station on Highway 52
trailing northeast through Minnesota.

Now a faded red barn, tumbledown outbuildings standing in cold
blue air, a hand-painted for sale sign, no one lives here now.
And up the hill from the highway a massive orphanage lies
abandoned as dozens of huge yellow brick buildings crumble.
Understand this place, hear the harmonies of its icy elements—
dissolution, loneliness, isolation.

Mayflower moving van passing by, people moving in to confront
the frozen land, here where a man can plan and with some grit
make something happen to this terrain where tilled land, farm
tools, sales shops, barns white and worn announce strong willed
men who work.

The sign Emma Crumby's Restaurant and Bakery announces
women work here, too, just as farm women do who scrub with cold
red hands, fingernails broken, hands that do not rest. The women
who occupy homes and work in the barns and fields, peer out
across acres of farmland now shiny with ice over snow.

Snow-filled furrows of harvested land expose the hard work
arranged by the hands of the people planting in this earth.
Far off a cluster of trees shelters a small ranch house with smoke
rising up signaling warmth, family, then over there and farther off
and closer by, scattered on this flat land are more groves, each
with one house, each a pledge to till this black and brown ocean of
lowland and highland.

These men and women together or alone, live distant from each other but remain close in purpose to be steady, steady, to work the land, listen to it, hear its discordant song of too much wind or snow or ice, not to give in to it, but to put by enough to stand against the freezing January winds, the blue sky gone gray, the snow falling.

Shades of Dying

A flock of sparrows
breaches the sky

above the brick
warehouse.

As they fly over,
their black shadows

soar straight down
the side of the building

into the brown earth
next to me in my car.

Is death so close
when dark shadows fall?

Gynecology

The nurse escorts me to the examination room that looks
like a cold empty shipping container headed out to sea.

She does not hand me a gown but leaves telling me the doctor
will be right in. Paper sheets spread on the table appear

to be great shrouds. Cold metal stirrups resembling handcuffs stick
out at angles at the end of the table. I begin thinking

about my 70-year-old mother, confused by Alzheimer's,
who wondered why her chest was covered with large bandages

appearing like flags warning women, Beware! Mary who died
in her 70s from breast cancer, and mother-in-law Merna who died

in her 90s from ovarian cancer. Finally, a light tap on the door and
in walks a young, sandy haired doctor looking like a surfer

at Myrtle Beach. He sits down on his stool, looks at his chart,
smiles, moves towards me and says, if I insist, he will do

my pap smear. He goes on to say because I am in my 70s
and my life expectancy is 80, my chances of getting cervical

cancer are slim. Stop! I hear Merna warning me from the grave.
His voice floats above me now like a dirge written in a minor key.

Calmly he sings his statistics to back up his recommendation.
Mary calls to me, Be leery. My heart is beating faster as he begins

to talk about the unnecessary breast exam. His voice floats higher
above me and all I hear is my mother crying out to me, Be careful!

I do not push back. Fuck him. How dare he tell me I am not viable? I will have my exams.

Women who reach 65 have a 71 percent chance of reaching 80 and a 34 percent chance of reaching 90. (The Hamilton Project.)

The Weeping Woman

The crying woman makes me weep
when I look at her contorted face

with its sharp angles, her large tears
falling white down her yellow face,

black green yellow purple hair
created with curving lines, her red

hat also in angles outlined in black
lines against a yellow and orange

striped background. Her dress is black
for mourning, her hands drawn up

to her face, to keep it from crumbling
and twitching. I see her open mouth

for her wailing to surge through.
She agonizes for all who die mercilessly.

She weeps at the loss of women with faces
and names—

Lyn, Harriet, Jeannie, Travis, Merna—
casualties of cancer—breast, uterine,

and ovarian—vile as any act of war.

The Weeping Woman, by Pablo Picasso (Spain) 1937.

Holy Ghosts in North Carolina

Swooshing by in the Carolinian,
I see through the red yellow orange leaves

between the dark brown limbs
ghosts dancing in the sharp cast

of noon light in countryside North Carolina.
White fields in fall, not snow and birch trees

as in the north in winter, but strange white fruit
gleaming against brown soil in the sunshine

while shadows run up and down the trunks
along the railroad tracks, great puffs of cotton

on bushes, white on brown and white on white,
cotton bulging and swinging by me—

leaping, then an open field with a row of white
bales each the size of a big red caboose

grand white beds so bewitching.
Will I be surprised by holy ghosts

soft warm white when slanted light comes
in my late afternoon—

bark of trunks glazed in orange and purple
glistening in a shadowed sun?

Tactical Fear in the Neighborhood

The photographer must see the beauty, so exacting
is the photo framed. The man and his cat stand

on a city street with nondescript buildings
behind them, a beat-up postal box plastered with fragments

of flyers—pink, yellow, blue, and green beside them.
The cat's green eyes shine as it peers at the sidewalk.

Its gray and tan fur wraps over the man's shoulder,
long black curls frame the sides of the man's face.

The man wears a bright gold sweatshirt over a brown tee-shirt.
His dark skin glows and his brown eyes pinch together

as he looks directly into the camera. Does the photographer see
the corners of the man's mouth turn slightly down,

both man and cat looking askance? The man's tense shoulders
belie the suspicion covering his face. He is on alert.

A white man walks behind him.

Photograph by Timothy Krause @ Flickr.
2015. William Victor, S.L.

74

Making Dinner

A cross section of this sliced carrot
reveals the core that fans out with life lines

to its outer layer, capillaries carrying water.
The color reminds me of the orange T-shirts

my daughter and her friends wear who gather
to radiate life lines when they rally to strengthen

gun laws. Earlier today the young woman
ahead of me in the check-out line at Harris Teeter

wore a black NRA T-shirt, on the back a skull
with pistols for crossbones.

She carried a holstered Glock on her right hip.

Smart Old Jewish Guys

I remember this old man. Here he needs
a shave, has large sunspots on his balding head,

ear lobes long with age. There he is, in blue plaid
under a dark gray jacket, hair longish. Trimmed

around his ears. Always took the subway to his
garment factory. (Gotta check up on the younger

ones running it now.) He still lives solo.
A penthouse overlooking Central Park. And a place

in the Hamptons of course. Never married.
Life too full with friends always over

in the kitchen to help prepare duck, the favorite!
Laugh and sip as they worked—him toasting them

with his glass of Gray Goose, but never before five.
On weekends, before heading out to the beach house,

always stopped in Southampton for his raspberry
frozen yogurt. The friends came, too. Talked

of their POW days, of being held by Nazi's, of getting
into Yale back when Jews were not accepted. They

watched PBS News Hour every Friday night, crowed
about politics, rode bikes in the morning, grabbed

walking sticks before they moved to the beach, took
a spin in his Town Car, out to the end…And yes, they

laughed and clapped each other on the back—old guys,
grinning because they outsmarted life.

After Photograph by Artis Rams @ Flickr. 2015. William Victor, S.L.

In the Hotel Waiting Room

Sitting in front of her, as she turns over
the pages of the newspaper folded open,
I can see what she is reading—the stock listings,

then Ameritrade, U.S. Auto Industry,
"Investors Wait—Watch," Morgan Stanley.
These keep her reading *The New York Times,*

this woman with arthritic hands grappling
with the newspaper, holding it up close to see.
I would guess she is in her late seventies,

early eighties, no rings on her fingers, nails
manicured in white pearl, brown hair set.
A handsome woman, she wears black and gold

clip-on earrings, black silk tailored shirt, slacks,
white jacket top-stitched at its mandarin collar
and sleeve edges, black leather handbag and loafers—

the finest contours. Now she moves to "Panel
Chastens Air Force Academy" and then "Grief
Spans from Afghanistan to Alabama." She keeps

reading. She is old, she has money, she reads.

Spring Tease at the Hardware

On a warm Monday in late April
an escalation of old folks surge
down the aisles of Lowes
with their carts full of yellow and purple
pansies, pink and white petunias,
red impatiens, geraniums.
Old guys in floppy tennis shoes
and navy-blue jogging suits squint
at labels on plant food
examine shiny trowels.
Women with fresh skirts
and dressy sweaters, their hair just so,
sashay loaded carts into check-out lanes,
rows and rows of men and women
waiting in line together,
going home to smell and feel the earth,
to loosen the soil in window boxes,
till small patches of garden
in front of their houses, work
dried manure into the soil,
mound plants into sinuous borders
in front of their azalea bushes,
water the plants, raise them up,
absorb the ample sex of it.

About the Author

Kay Bosgraaf was raised in Hudsonville, Michigan, and now lives in Durham, North Carolina. She has B.A., M.A., and Ph.D. degrees. Her publications include two books entitled *Song of Serenity: Poems* and *The Fence Lesson: Poems* as well as a chapbook entitled *Blue Eyes and Homburg Hats: Poems.* Individual poems have appeared in numerous journals and literary magazines. She was recently the recipient of a MacDowell Colony residency and has had two residencies at Vermont Studio Center. Her teaching has included some years at Michigan State University, seven years at Lincoln Memorial University in Appalachia, and, her longest tenure, at Montgomery College in Rockville, Maryland. After a lifetime of full-time teaching of creative writing, rhetoric and composition, and literature, she now writes and teaches creative writing as an adjunct professor at regional colleges and universities.

Kelsay Books

www.ingramcontent.com/pod-product-compliance
Lightning Source LLC
Chambersburg PA
CBHW031004090426
42737CB00008B/675